THIS BOOK BELONGS TO:

_____
_____
_____

EMERGENCY CONTACT:

_____
_____
_____

Copyright © Teresa Rother

All rights reserved. No part of this publication may be reproduced, distributed, or transmitted in any form or by any means, including photocopy, recording, or other electronic or mechanical methods.

DEDICATION

This Hiking Log Book is dedicated to hiking and backpacking enthusiasts who want to document their journey. Preparing and organizing will help you enjoy your adventure and allow you to keep a record of all the details.

You are my inspiration for producing this book and I'm honored to be a part of your record-keeping and hiking experience.

HOW TO USE THIS BOOK

This Hiking Log Book will help guide you by accurately recording each hike.

Here are examples of tracking and prompts for you to fill in and write the details of your experience: hiking trail, location, start time, and much more.

Fill in the following information:

1. Date
2. Trail/Location
3. Start time, End time, Duration
4. Terrain, elevation, distance
5. Gear, food, water
6. Onsite facilities, water availability
7. Companion list
8. Trail condition and weather
9. Phone reception/carrier
10. Rate trail difficulty
11. Overall rating
12. Notes

HIKING LOG

Date

Hike/Trail Name	Location	

Start Time	End Time	Duration

Terrain	Elevation Gain/Loss	Distance

Gear	Food/Water	Onsite Facilities/Water
		Companions

Trail Conditions	Weather	Phone Reception/Carrier
		Difficulty
		☆ ☆ ☆ ☆ ☆
		Overall Rating
		☆ ☆ ☆ ☆ ☆

Notes

 # HIKING LOG

Date

Hike/Trail Name	Location	

Start Time	End Time	Duration

Terrain	Elevation Gain/Loss	Distance

Gear	Food/Water	Onsite Facilities/Water
		Companions

Trail Conditions	Weather	Phone Reception/Carrier
		Difficulty
		☆ ☆ ☆ ☆ ☆
		Overall Rating
		☆ ☆ ☆ ☆ ☆

Notes

HIKING LOG

Date

Hike/Trail Name	Location	
Start Time	End Time	Duration
Terrain	Elevation Gain/Loss	Distance
Gear	Food/Water	Onsite Facilities/Water
		Companions
Trail Conditions	Weather	Phone Reception/Carrier
		Difficulty
		☆ ☆ ☆ ☆ ☆
		Overall Rating
		☆ ☆ ☆ ☆ ☆

Notes

HIKING LOG

		Date	
Hike/Trail Name		Location	
Start Time	End Time		Duration
Terrain	Elevation Gain/Loss		Distance
Gear	Food/Water		Onsite Facilities/Water
			Companions
Trail Conditions	Weather		Phone Reception/Carrier
	☀️ ⛅ ☁️ 🌬️ 🌧️ ⛈️ ❄️		Difficulty ☆☆☆☆☆
			Overall Rating ☆☆☆☆☆
Notes			

HIKING LOG

Date

Hike/Trail Name	Location	

Start Time	End Time	Duration

Terrain	Elevation Gain/Loss	Distance

Gear	Food/Water	Onsite Facilities/Water
		Companions

Trail Conditions	Weather	Phone Reception/Carrier
		Difficulty
		☆ ☆ ☆ ☆ ☆
		Overall Rating
		☆ ☆ ☆ ☆ ☆

Notes

HIKING LOG

Date

Hike/Trail Name	Location	
Start Time	End Time	Duration
Terrain	Elevation Gain/Loss	Distance
Gear	Food/Water	Onsite Facilities/Water
		Companions
Trail Conditions	Weather	Phone Reception/Carrier
		Difficulty ☆☆☆☆☆
		Overall Rating ☆☆☆☆☆

Notes

HIKING LOG

	Date
Hike/Trail Name	**Location**
Start Time	**End Time**	**Duration**
Terrain	**Elevation Gain/Loss**	**Distance**
Gear	**Food/Water**	**Onsite Facilities/Water**
		Companions
Trail Conditions	**Weather**	**Phone Reception/Carrier**
		Difficulty
		☆☆☆☆☆
		Overall Rating
		☆☆☆☆☆
Notes		

HIKING LOG

Date

Hike/Trail Name	Location	

Start Time	End Time	Duration

Terrain	Elevation Gain/Loss	Distance

Gear	Food/Water	Onsite Facilities/Water
		Companions

Trail Conditions	Weather	Phone Reception/Carrier
		Difficulty
		☆☆☆☆☆
		Overall Rating
		☆☆☆☆☆

Notes

HIKING LOG

Date

Hike/Trail Name	Location	

Start Time	End Time	Duration

Terrain	Elevation Gain/Loss	Distance

Gear	Food/Water	Onsite Facilities/Water
		Companions

Trail Conditions	Weather	Phone Reception/Carrier
		Difficulty
		☆ ☆ ☆ ☆ ☆
		Overall Rating
		☆ ☆ ☆ ☆ ☆

Notes

 HIKING LOG

Date

Hike/Trail Name	Location	

Start Time	End Time	Duration

Terrain	Elevation Gain/Loss	Distance

Gear	Food/Water	Onsite Facilities/Water
		Companions

Trail Conditions	Weather	Phone Reception/Carrier
	☀ ⛅ ☁ 🌬 ☔ ⛈ ❄	
		Difficulty
		☆☆☆☆☆
		Overall Rating
		☆☆☆☆☆

Notes

HIKING LOG

Date

Hike/Trail Name	Location	

Start Time	End Time	Duration

Terrain	Elevation Gain/Loss	Distance

Gear	Food/Water	Onsite Facilities/Water
		Companions

Trail Conditions	Weather	Phone Reception/Carrier
		Difficulty
		☆ ☆ ☆ ☆ ☆
		Overall Rating
		☆ ☆ ☆ ☆ ☆

Notes

HIKING LOG	Date	
Hike/Trail Name	Location	
Start Time	End Time	Duration
Terrain	Elevation Gain/Loss	Distance
Gear	Food/Water	Onsite Facilities/Water
		Companions
Trail Conditions	Weather	Phone Reception/Carrier
		Difficulty ☆☆☆☆☆
		Overall Rating ☆☆☆☆☆
Notes		

HIKING LOG

Date	

Hike/Trail Name	Location	
Start Time	End Time	Duration
Terrain	Elevation Gain/Loss	Distance
Gear	Food/Water	Onsite Facilities/Water
		Companions
Trail Conditions	Weather	Phone Reception/Carrier
		Difficulty ☆☆☆☆☆
		Overall Rating ☆☆☆☆☆
Notes		

HIKING LOG

	Date
Hike/Trail Name	Location
Start Time	End Time	Duration
Terrain	Elevation Gain/Loss	Distance
Gear	Food/Water	Onsite Facilities/Water
		Companions
Trail Conditions	Weather	Phone Reception/Carrier
		Difficulty
		☆☆☆☆☆
		Overall Rating
		☆☆☆☆☆

Notes

HIKING LOG

		Date	
Hike/Trail Name		Location	
Start Time	End Time		Duration
Terrain	Elevation Gain/Loss		Distance
Gear	Food/Water		Onsite Facilities/Water
			Companions
Trail Conditions	Weather		Phone Reception/Carrier
			Difficulty
			☆ ☆ ☆ ☆ ☆
			Overall Rating
			☆ ☆ ☆ ☆ ☆
	Notes		

 **HIKING LOG**	Date

Hike/Trail Name	Location	

Start Time	End Time	Duration

Terrain	Elevation Gain/Loss	Distance

Gear	Food/Water	Onsite Facilities/Water
		Companions

Trail Conditions	Weather	Phone Reception/Carrier
	☀ 🌤 ☁ 🌬 🌧 ⛈ ❄	
		Difficulty
		☆☆☆☆☆
		Overall Rating
		☆☆☆☆☆

Notes

HIKING LOG

Date

Hike/Trail Name	Location	

Start Time	End Time	Duration

Terrain	Elevation Gain/Loss	Distance

Gear	Food/Water	Onsite Facilities/Water
		Companions

Trail Conditions	Weather	Phone Reception/Carrier
	☀ ⛅ ☁ 🌬 🌧 ⛈ ❄	
		Difficulty
		☆☆☆☆☆
		Overall Rating
		☆☆☆☆☆

Notes

HIKING LOG	Date	
Hike/Trail Name	Location	
Start Time	End Time	Duration
Terrain	Elevation Gain/Loss	Distance
Gear	Food/Water	Onsite Facilities/Water
		Companions
Trail Conditions	Weather	Phone Reception/Carrier
		Difficulty ☆☆☆☆☆
		Overall Rating ☆☆☆☆☆
Notes		

HIKING LOG

Date

Hike/Trail Name	Location	
Start Time	End Time	Duration
Terrain	Elevation Gain/Loss	Distance
Gear	Food/Water	Onsite Facilities/Water
		Companions
Trail Conditions	Weather	Phone Reception/Carrier
		Difficulty ☆ ☆ ☆ ☆ ☆
		Overall Rating ☆ ☆ ☆ ☆ ☆

Notes

HIKING LOG

		Date

Hike/Trail Name	Location	

Start Time	End Time	Duration

Terrain	Elevation Gain/Loss	Distance

Gear	Food/Water	Onsite Facilities/Water
		Companions

Trail Conditions	Weather	Phone Reception/Carrier
	☀ 🌤 ☁ 💨 🌧 ⛈ ❄	
		Difficulty
		☆☆☆☆☆
		Overall Rating
		☆☆☆☆☆

Notes

HIKING LOG

Date

Hike/Trail Name	Location	
Start Time	End Time	Duration
Terrain	Elevation Gain/Loss	Distance
Gear	Food/Water	Onsite Facilities/Water
		Companions
Trail Conditions	Weather	Phone Reception/Carrier
		Difficulty ☆☆☆☆☆
		Overall Rating ☆☆☆☆☆

Notes

 HIKING LOG

		Date
Hike/Trail Name	Location	
Start Time	End Time	Duration
Terrain	Elevation Gain/Loss	Distance
Gear	Food/Water	Onsite Facilities/Water
		Companions
Trail Conditions	Weather	Phone Reception/Carrier
		Difficulty ☆☆☆☆☆
		Overall Rating ☆☆☆☆☆
Notes		

HIKING LOG

Date	

Hike/Trail Name	Location	

Start Time	End Time	Duration

Terrain	Elevation Gain/Loss	Distance

Gear	Food/Water	Onsite Facilities/Water
		Companions

Trail Conditions	Weather	Phone Reception/Carrier
		Difficulty
		☆ ☆ ☆ ☆ ☆
		Overall Rating
		☆ ☆ ☆ ☆ ☆

Notes

HIKING LOG

Date	

Hike/Trail Name	Location

Start Time	End Time	Duration

Terrain	Elevation Gain/Loss	Distance

Gear	Food/Water	Onsite Facilities/Water
		Companions

Trail Conditions	Weather	Phone Reception/Carrier
		Difficulty
		☆☆☆☆☆
		Overall Rating
		☆☆☆☆☆

Notes

HIKING LOG

Date	

Hike/Trail Name	Location	

Start Time	End Time	Duration

Terrain	Elevation Gain/Loss	Distance

Gear	Food/Water	Onsite Facilities/Water
		Companions

Trail Conditions	Weather	Phone Reception/Carrier
	☀ ⛅ ☁ 🌬	
	🌧 ⛈ ❄	
		Difficulty
		☆ ☆ ☆ ☆ ☆
		Overall Rating
		☆ ☆ ☆ ☆ ☆

Notes

HIKING LOG

		Date
Hike/Trail Name	Location	
Start Time	End Time	Duration
Terrain	Elevation Gain/Loss	Distance
Gear	Food/Water	Onsite Facilities/Water
		Companions
Trail Conditions	Weather	Phone Reception/Carrier
	☀ 🌤 ☁ 💨 🌧 ⛈ 🌨	
		Difficulty
		☆☆☆☆☆
		Overall Rating
		☆☆☆☆☆
Notes		

HIKING LOG

Date

Hike/Trail Name	Location	

Start Time	End Time	Duration

Terrain	Elevation Gain/Loss	Distance

Gear	Food/Water	Onsite Facilities/Water
		Companions

Trail Conditions	Weather	Phone Reception/Carrier
		Difficulty
		☆ ☆ ☆ ☆ ☆
		Overall Rating
		☆ ☆ ☆ ☆ ☆

Notes	

HIKING LOG

Date

Hike/Trail Name	Location	

Start Time	End Time	Duration

Terrain	Elevation Gain/Loss	Distance

Gear	Food/Water	Onsite Facilities/Water
		Companions

Trail Conditions	Weather	Phone Reception/Carrier
		Difficulty
		☆ ☆ ☆ ☆ ☆
		Overall Rating
		☆ ☆ ☆ ☆ ☆

Notes

HIKING LOG

Date

Hike/Trail Name	Location	

Start Time	End Time	Duration

Terrain	Elevation Gain/Loss	Distance

Gear	Food/Water	Onsite Facilities/Water
		Companions

Trail Conditions	Weather	Phone Reception/Carrier
		Difficulty
		☆ ☆ ☆ ☆ ☆
		Overall Rating
		☆ ☆ ☆ ☆ ☆

Notes

HIKING LOG

		Date
Hike/Trail Name	Location	
Start Time	End Time	Duration
Terrain	Elevation Gain/Loss	Distance
Gear	Food/Water	Onsite Facilities/Water
		Companions
Trail Conditions	Weather	Phone Reception/Carrier
	☀ 🌤 ☁ 🌬 🌧 ⛈ ❄	
		Difficulty ☆☆☆☆☆
		Overall Rating ☆☆☆☆☆
Notes		

HIKING LOG

Date

Hike/Trail Name	Location	

Start Time	End Time	Duration

Terrain	Elevation Gain/Loss	Distance

Gear	Food/Water	Onsite Facilities/Water
		Companions

Trail Conditions	Weather	Phone Reception/Carrier
		Difficulty
		☆☆☆☆☆
		Overall Rating
		☆☆☆☆☆

Notes

HIKING LOG

		Date

Hike/Trail Name	Location	

Start Time	End Time	Duration

Terrain	Elevation Gain/Loss	Distance

Gear	Food/Water	Onsite Facilities/Water
		Companions

Trail Conditions	Weather	Phone Reception/Carrier
	☀ ⛅ ☁ 🌬	
	🌧 ⛈ ❄	
		Difficulty
		☆☆☆☆☆
		Overall Rating
		☆☆☆☆☆

Notes

HIKING LOG

		Date	
Hike/Trail Name		Location	
Start Time	End Time		Duration
Terrain	Elevation Gain/Loss		Distance
Gear	Food/Water		Onsite Facilities/Water
			Companions
Trail Conditions	Weather		Phone Reception/Carrier
			Difficulty ☆☆☆☆☆
			Overall Rating ☆☆☆☆☆
Notes			

HIKING LOG

		Date
Hike/Trail Name	Location	
Start Time	End Time	Duration
Terrain	Elevation Gain/Loss	Distance
Gear	Food/Water	Onsite Facilities/Water
		Companions
Trail Conditions	Weather	Phone Reception/Carrier
		Difficulty ☆☆☆☆☆
		Overall Rating ☆☆☆☆☆
Notes		

HIKING LOG

Date	

Hike/Trail Name	Location	

Start Time	End Time	Duration

Terrain	Elevation Gain/Loss	Distance

Gear	Food/Water	Onsite Facilities/Water
		Companions

Trail Conditions	Weather	Phone Reception/Carrier
		Difficulty
		☆ ☆ ☆ ☆ ☆
		Overall Rating
		☆ ☆ ☆ ☆ ☆

Notes

HIKING LOG	Date	
Hike/Trail Name	Location	
Start Time	End Time	Duration
Terrain	Elevation Gain/Loss	Distance
Gear	Food/Water	Onsite Facilities/Water
		Companions
Trail Conditions	Weather	Phone Reception/Carrier
		Difficulty
		☆☆☆☆☆
		Overall Rating
		☆☆☆☆☆
Notes		

 # HIKING LOG

	Date

Hike/Trail Name	Location	

Start Time	End Time	Duration

Terrain	Elevation Gain/Loss	Distance

Gear	Food/Water	Onsite Facilities/Water
		Companions

Trail Conditions	Weather	Phone Reception/Carrier
		Difficulty
		☆☆☆☆☆
		Overall Rating
		☆☆☆☆☆

Notes

 **HIKING LOG** | Date

Hike/Trail Name	Location	
Start Time	End Time	Duration
Terrain	Elevation Gain/Loss	Distance
Gear	Food/Water	Onsite Facilities/Water
		Companions
Trail Conditions	Weather	Phone Reception/Carrier
		Difficulty
		☆☆☆☆☆
		Overall Rating
		☆☆☆☆☆
Notes		

HIKING LOG

Date

Hike/Trail Name	Location	
Start Time	End Time	Duration
Terrain	Elevation Gain/Loss	Distance
Gear	Food/Water	Onsite Facilities/Water
		Companions
Trail Conditions	Weather	Phone Reception/Carrier
		Difficulty
		☆ ☆ ☆ ☆ ☆
		Overall Rating
		☆ ☆ ☆ ☆ ☆
Notes		

HIKING LOG

Date	

Hike/Trail Name	Location

Start Time	End Time	Duration

Terrain	Elevation Gain/Loss	Distance

Gear	Food/Water	Onsite Facilities/Water
		Companions

Trail Conditions	Weather	Phone Reception/Carrier
	☀ 🌤 ☁ 🌬 🌧 ⛈ 🌨	
		Difficulty
		☆ ☆ ☆ ☆ ☆
		Overall Rating
		☆ ☆ ☆ ☆ ☆

Notes

HIKING LOG

Date	

Hike/Trail Name	Location	

Start Time	End Time	Duration

Terrain	Elevation Gain/Loss	Distance

Gear	Food/Water	Onsite Facilities/Water
		Companions

Trail Conditions	Weather	Phone Reception/Carrier
	☀ ⛅ ☁ 🌬 🌧 ⛈ ❄	
		Difficulty
		☆ ☆ ☆ ☆ ☆
		Overall Rating
		☆ ☆ ☆ ☆ ☆

Notes

HIKING LOG

		Date
Hike/Trail Name	Location	
Start Time	End Time	Duration
Terrain	Elevation Gain/Loss	Distance
Gear	Food/Water	Onsite Facilities/Water
		Companions
Trail Conditions	Weather	Phone Reception/Carrier
		Difficulty ☆☆☆☆☆
		Overall Rating ☆☆☆☆☆
Notes		

HIKING LOG

	Date

Hike/Trail Name	Location	

Start Time	End Time	Duration

Terrain	Elevation Gain/Loss	Distance

Gear	Food/Water	Onsite Facilities/Water
		Companions

Trail Conditions	Weather	Phone Reception/Carrier
		Difficulty
		☆ ☆ ☆ ☆ ☆
		Overall Rating
		☆ ☆ ☆ ☆ ☆

Notes

HIKING LOG

Date	

Hike/Trail Name	Location	
Start Time	End Time	Duration
Terrain	Elevation Gain/Loss	Distance
Gear	Food/Water	Onsite Facilities/Water
		Companions
Trail Conditions	Weather	Phone Reception/Carrier
	☀ ⛅ ☁ 🌬 🌧 ⛈ ❄	
		Difficulty
		☆☆☆☆☆
		Overall Rating
		☆☆☆☆☆
Notes		

HIKING LOG

Date

Hike/Trail Name	Location	

Start Time	End Time	Duration

Terrain	Elevation Gain/Loss	Distance

Gear	Food/Water	Onsite Facilities/Water
		Companions

Trail Conditions	Weather	Phone Reception/Carrier
		Difficulty
		☆ ☆ ☆ ☆ ☆
		Overall Rating
		☆ ☆ ☆ ☆ ☆

Notes

HIKING LOG	Date	
Hike/Trail Name	Location	
Start Time	End Time	Duration
Terrain	Elevation Gain/Loss	Distance
Gear	Food/Water	Onsite Facilities/Water
		Companions
Trail Conditions	Weather	Phone Reception/Carrier
		Difficulty ☆☆☆☆☆
		Overall Rating ☆☆☆☆☆
Notes		

HIKING LOG

Date

Hike/Trail Name	Location	

Start Time	End Time	Duration

Terrain	Elevation Gain/Loss	Distance

Gear	Food/Water	Onsite Facilities/Water
		Companions

Trail Conditions	Weather	Phone Reception/Carrier
	☀ ⛅ ☁ 🌬 🌧 ⛈ ❄	
		Difficulty
		☆☆☆☆☆
		Overall Rating
		☆☆☆☆☆

Notes

HIKING LOG

Date

Hike/Trail Name	Location	

Start Time	End Time	Duration

Terrain	Elevation Gain/Loss	Distance

Gear	Food/Water	Onsite Facilities/Water
		Companions

Trail Conditions	Weather	Phone Reception/Carrier
		Difficulty
		☆ ☆ ☆ ☆ ☆
		Overall Rating
		☆ ☆ ☆ ☆ ☆

Notes

HIKING LOG

Date

Hike/Trail Name	Location	

Start Time	End Time	Duration

Terrain	Elevation Gain/Loss	Distance

Gear	Food/Water	Onsite Facilities/Water
		Companions

Trail Conditions	Weather	Phone Reception/Carrier
	☀️ ⛅ ☁️ 🌬️ 🌧️ ⛈️ ❄️	
		Difficulty
		☆☆☆☆☆
		Overall Rating
		☆☆☆☆☆

Notes

HIKING LOG

Date	

Hike/Trail Name	Location

Start Time	End Time	Duration

Terrain	Elevation Gain/Loss	Distance

Gear	Food/Water	Onsite Facilities/Water
		Companions

Trail Conditions	Weather	Phone Reception/Carrier
	☀ ⛅ ☁ 🌬 🌧 ⛈ ❄	
		Difficulty
		☆☆☆☆☆
		Overall Rating
		☆☆☆☆☆

Notes

HIKING LOG

Date

Hike/Trail Name	Location	
Start Time	End Time	Duration
Terrain	Elevation Gain/Loss	Distance
Gear	Food/Water	Onsite Facilities/Water
		Companions
Trail Conditions	Weather	Phone Reception/Carrier
		Difficulty ☆☆☆☆☆
		Overall Rating ☆☆☆☆☆

Notes

HIKING LOG	Date

Hike/Trail Name	Location

Start Time	End Time	Duration

Terrain	Elevation Gain/Loss	Distance

Gear	Food/Water	Onsite Facilities/Water
		Companions

Trail Conditions	Weather	Phone Reception/Carrier
		Difficulty ☆☆☆☆☆
		Overall Rating ☆☆☆☆☆

Notes

HIKING LOG

Date

Hike/Trail Name	Location	

Start Time	End Time	Duration

Terrain	Elevation Gain/Loss	Distance

Gear	Food/Water	Onsite Facilities/Water
		Companions

Trail Conditions	Weather	Phone Reception/Carrier
		Difficulty
		☆ ☆ ☆ ☆ ☆
		Overall Rating
		☆ ☆ ☆ ☆ ☆

Notes

HIKING LOG

		Date
Hike/Trail Name	Location	
Start Time	End Time	Duration
Terrain	Elevation Gain/Loss	Distance
Gear	Food/Water	Onsite Facilities/Water
		Companions
Trail Conditions	Weather	Phone Reception/Carrier
		Difficulty ☆☆☆☆☆
		Overall Rating ☆☆☆☆☆
Notes		

HIKING LOG

Date

Hike/Trail Name	Location	

Start Time	End Time	Duration

Terrain	Elevation Gain/Loss	Distance

Gear	Food/Water	Onsite Facilities/Water
		Companions

Trail Conditions	Weather	Phone Reception/Carrier
		Difficulty
		☆ ☆ ☆ ☆ ☆
		Overall Rating
		☆ ☆ ☆ ☆ ☆

Notes

HIKING LOG	Date

Hike/Trail Name	Location	

Start Time	End Time	Duration

Terrain	Elevation Gain/Loss	Distance

Gear	Food/Water	Onsite Facilities/Water
		Companions

Trail Conditions	Weather	Phone Reception/Carrier
	☀ 🌤 ☁ 🌬 🌧 ⛈ ❄	
		Difficulty
		☆☆☆☆☆
		Overall Rating
		☆☆☆☆☆

Notes

HIKING LOG

Date	

Hike/Trail Name	Location

Start Time	End Time	Duration

Terrain	Elevation Gain/Loss	Distance

Gear	Food/Water	Onsite Facilities/Water
		Companions

Trail Conditions	Weather	Phone Reception/Carrier
		Difficulty
		☆ ☆ ☆ ☆ ☆
		Overall Rating
		☆ ☆ ☆ ☆ ☆

Notes

HIKING LOG | Date

Hike/Trail Name	Location	
Start Time	End Time	Duration
Terrain	Elevation Gain/Loss	Distance
Gear	Food/Water	Onsite Facilities/Water
		Companions
Trail Conditions	Weather	Phone Reception/Carrier
		Difficulty
		☆☆☆☆☆
		Overall Rating
		☆☆☆☆☆
Notes		

HIKING LOG

Date

Hike/Trail Name	Location	
Start Time	End Time	Duration
Terrain	Elevation Gain/Loss	Distance
Gear	Food/Water	Onsite Facilities/Water
		Companions
Trail Conditions	Weather	Phone Reception/Carrier
		Difficulty ☆☆☆☆☆
		Overall Rating ☆☆☆☆☆
Notes		

HIKING LOG

Date	

Hike/Trail Name	Location	

Start Time	End Time	Duration

Terrain	Elevation Gain/Loss	Distance

Gear	Food/Water	Onsite Facilities/Water
		Companions
Trail Conditions	Weather	Phone Reception/Carrier
		Difficulty
		☆☆☆☆☆
		Overall Rating
		☆☆☆☆☆

Notes

HIKING LOG

Date	

Hike/Trail Name	Location	

Start Time	End Time	Duration

Terrain	Elevation Gain/Loss	Distance

Gear	Food/Water	Onsite Facilities/Water
		Companions

Trail Conditions	Weather	Phone Reception/Carrier
		Difficulty
		☆ ☆ ☆ ☆ ☆
		Overall Rating
		☆ ☆ ☆ ☆ ☆

Notes

HIKING LOG

		Date	
Hike/Trail Name		Location	
Start Time	End Time		Duration
Terrain	Elevation Gain/Loss		Distance
Gear	Food/Water		Onsite Facilities/Water
			Companions
Trail Conditions	Weather		Phone Reception/Carrier
			Difficulty
			☆☆☆☆☆
			Overall Rating
			☆☆☆☆☆
Notes			

HIKING LOG

	Date

Hike/Trail Name	Location	

Start Time	End Time	Duration

Terrain	Elevation Gain/Loss	Distance

Gear	Food/Water	Onsite Facilities/Water
		Companions

Trail Conditions	Weather	Phone Reception/Carrier
		Difficulty
		☆ ☆ ☆ ☆ ☆
		Overall Rating
		☆ ☆ ☆ ☆ ☆

Notes

HIKING LOG

		Date
Hike/Trail Name	Location	
Start Time	End Time	Duration
Terrain	Elevation Gain/Loss	Distance
Gear	Food/Water	Onsite Facilities/Water
		Companions
Trail Conditions	Weather	Phone Reception/Carrier
		Difficulty ☆☆☆☆☆
		Overall Rating ☆☆☆☆☆
Notes		

HIKING LOG

Date

Hike/Trail Name	Location	

Start Time	End Time	Duration

Terrain	Elevation Gain/Loss	Distance

Gear	Food/Water	Onsite Facilities/Water
		Companions

Trail Conditions	Weather	Phone Reception/Carrier
	☀ ⛅ ☁ 🌬 🌧 ⛈ ❄	
		Difficulty
		☆☆☆☆☆
		Overall Rating
		☆☆☆☆☆

Notes

HIKING LOG

Date

Hike/Trail Name	Location	

Start Time	End Time	Duration

Terrain	Elevation Gain/Loss	Distance

Gear	Food/Water	Onsite Facilities/Water
		Companions

Trail Conditions	Weather	Phone Reception/Carrier
	☀ 🌤 ☁ 🌬 🌧 ⛈ ❄	
		Difficulty
		☆ ☆ ☆ ☆ ☆
		Overall Rating
		☆ ☆ ☆ ☆ ☆

Notes

HIKING LOG | Date

Hike/Trail Name	Location	
Start Time	End Time	Duration
Terrain	Elevation Gain/Loss	Distance
Gear	Food/Water	Onsite Facilities/Water
		Companions
Trail Conditions	Weather	Phone Reception/Carrier
	☀️ ⛅ ☁️🌬️ 🌧️ ⛈️ 🌨️	
		Difficulty
		☆☆☆☆☆
		Overall Rating
		☆☆☆☆☆
Notes		

HIKING LOG	Date	
Hike/Trail Name	Location	
Start Time	End Time	Duration
Terrain	Elevation Gain/Loss	Distance
Gear	Food/Water	Onsite Facilities/Water
		Companions
Trail Conditions	Weather	Phone Reception/Carrier
		Difficulty
		☆☆☆☆☆
		Overall Rating
		☆☆☆☆☆
Notes		

HIKING LOG

Date

Hike/Trail Name	Location	

Start Time	End Time	Duration

Terrain	Elevation Gain/Loss	Distance

Gear	Food/Water	Onsite Facilities/Water
		Companions

Trail Conditions	Weather	Phone Reception/Carrier
	☀ ⛅ ☁ 🌬 🌧 ⛈ ❄	
		Difficulty
		☆ ☆ ☆ ☆ ☆
		Overall Rating
		☆ ☆ ☆ ☆ ☆

Notes

 HIKING LOG	Date	
Hike/Trail Name	Location	

Start Time	End Time	Duration

Terrain	Elevation Gain/Loss	Distance

Gear	Food/Water	Onsite Facilities/Water
		Companions

Trail Conditions	Weather	Phone Reception/Carrier
		Difficulty
		☆ ☆ ☆ ☆ ☆
		Overall Rating
		☆ ☆ ☆ ☆ ☆

Notes

HIKING LOG

Date

Hike/Trail Name	Location	
Start Time	End Time	Duration
Terrain	Elevation Gain/Loss	Distance
Gear	Food/Water	Onsite Facilities/Water
		Companions
Trail Conditions	Weather	Phone Reception/Carrier
		Difficulty
		☆ ☆ ☆ ☆ ☆
		Overall Rating
		☆ ☆ ☆ ☆ ☆
Notes		

HIKING LOG

Date	

Hike/Trail Name	Location

Start Time	End Time	Duration

Terrain	Elevation Gain/Loss	Distance

Gear	Food/Water	Onsite Facilities/Water
		Companions

Trail Conditions	Weather	Phone Reception/Carrier
		Difficulty
		☆☆☆☆☆
		Overall Rating
		☆☆☆☆☆

Notes

HIKING LOG

Date

Hike/Trail Name	Location	

Start Time	End Time	Duration

Terrain	Elevation Gain/Loss	Distance

Gear	Food/Water	Onsite Facilities/Water
		Companions

Trail Conditions	Weather	Phone Reception/Carrier
		Difficulty
		☆☆☆☆☆
		Overall Rating
		☆☆☆☆☆

Notes

HIKING LOG

		Date
Hike/Trail Name	Location	
Start Time	End Time	Duration
Terrain	Elevation Gain/Loss	Distance
Gear	Food/Water	Onsite Facilities/Water
		Companions
Trail Conditions	Weather	Phone Reception/Carrier
	☀ ⛅ ☁ 🌬 🌧 ⛈ 🌨	
		Difficulty
		☆☆☆☆☆
		Overall Rating
		☆☆☆☆☆
Notes		

HIKING LOG

	Date

Hike/Trail Name	Location	

Start Time	End Time	Duration

Terrain	Elevation Gain/Loss	Distance

Gear	Food/Water	Onsite Facilities/Water
		Companions

Trail Conditions	Weather	Phone Reception/Carrier
		Difficulty
		☆ ☆ ☆ ☆ ☆
		Overall Rating
		☆ ☆ ☆ ☆ ☆

Notes

		Date
Hike/Trail Name	**Location**	
Start Time	**End Time**	**Duration**
Terrain	**Elevation Gain/Loss**	**Distance**
Gear	**Food/Water**	**Onsite Facilities/Water**
		Companions
Trail Conditions	**Weather**	**Phone Reception/Carrier**
		Difficulty ☆☆☆☆☆
		Overall Rating ☆☆☆☆☆
Notes		

HIKING LOG

Date

Hike/Trail Name	Location	

Start Time	End Time	Duration

Terrain	Elevation Gain/Loss	Distance

Gear	Food/Water	Onsite Facilities/Water
		Companions

Trail Conditions	Weather	Phone Reception/Carrier
		Difficulty
		☆ ☆ ☆ ☆ ☆
		Overall Rating
		☆ ☆ ☆ ☆ ☆

Notes

HIKING LOG | Date

Hike/Trail Name	Location	
Start Time	End Time	Duration
Terrain	Elevation Gain/Loss	Distance
Gear	Food/Water	Onsite Facilities/Water
		Companions
Trail Conditions	Weather	Phone Reception/Carrier
		Difficulty
		☆☆☆☆☆
		Overall Rating
		☆☆☆☆☆
Notes		

HIKING LOG

Date

Hike/Trail Name	Location	

Start Time	End Time	Duration

Terrain	Elevation Gain/Loss	Distance

Gear	Food/Water	Onsite Facilities/Water
		Companions

Trail Conditions	Weather	Phone Reception/Carrier
		Difficulty
		☆ ☆ ☆ ☆ ☆
		Overall Rating
		☆ ☆ ☆ ☆ ☆

Notes

 **HIKING LOG** | Date

Hike/Trail Name	Location	

Start Time	End Time	Duration

Terrain	Elevation Gain/Loss	Distance

Gear	Food/Water	Onsite Facilities/Water
		Companions

Trail Conditions	Weather	Phone Reception/Carrier
		Difficulty
		☆☆☆☆☆
		Overall Rating
		☆☆☆☆☆

Notes

HIKING LOG

Date

Hike/Trail Name	Location	
Start Time	End Time	Duration
Terrain	Elevation Gain/Loss	Distance
Gear	Food/Water	Onsite Facilities/Water
		Companions
Trail Conditions	Weather	Phone Reception/Carrier
	☀ ⛅ ☁ 🌬 🌧 ⛈ ❄	
		Difficulty
		☆☆☆☆☆
		Overall Rating
		☆☆☆☆☆
	Notes	

HIKING LOG | Date

Hike/Trail Name	Location	
Start Time	End Time	Duration
Terrain	Elevation Gain/Loss	Distance
Gear	Food/Water	Onsite Facilities/Water
		Companions
Trail Conditions	Weather	Phone Reception/Carrier
		Difficulty
		☆☆☆☆☆
		Overall Rating
		☆☆☆☆☆

Notes

HIKING LOG

Date	

Hike/Trail Name	Location	

Start Time	End Time	Duration

Terrain	Elevation Gain/Loss	Distance

Gear	Food/Water	Onsite Facilities/Water
		Companions

Trail Conditions	Weather	Phone Reception/Carrier
		Difficulty ☆☆☆☆☆
		Overall Rating ☆☆☆☆☆

Notes

HIKING LOG | Date

Hike/Trail Name	Location	
Start Time	End Time	Duration
Terrain	Elevation Gain/Loss	Distance
Gear	Food/Water	Onsite Facilities/Water
		Companions
Trail Conditions	Weather	Phone Reception/Carrier
		Difficulty
		☆☆☆☆☆
		Overall Rating
		☆☆☆☆☆
Notes		

HIKING LOG

Date	

Hike/Trail Name	Location

Start Time	End Time	Duration

Terrain	Elevation Gain/Loss	Distance

Gear	Food/Water	Onsite Facilities/Water
		Companions

Trail Conditions	Weather	Phone Reception/Carrier
	☀ ⛅ ☁ 🌧 ⛈ ❄	
		Difficulty
		☆ ☆ ☆ ☆ ☆
		Overall Rating
		☆ ☆ ☆ ☆ ☆

Notes

HIKING LOG	Date

Hike/Trail Name	Location	

Start Time	End Time	Duration

Terrain	Elevation Gain/Loss	Distance

Gear	Food/Water	Onsite Facilities/Water
		Companions

Trail Conditions	Weather	Phone Reception/Carrier
	☀️ ⛅ ☁️ 🌬️ 🌧️ ⛈️ ❄️	
		Difficulty
		☆☆☆☆☆
		Overall Rating
		☆☆☆☆☆

Notes

HIKING LOG

Date

Hike/Trail Name	Location	

Start Time	End Time	Duration

Terrain	Elevation Gain/Loss	Distance

Gear	Food/Water	Onsite Facilities/Water
		Companions

Trail Conditions	Weather	Phone Reception/Carrier
	☀ ⛅ ☁ 🌬 🌧 ⛈ ❄	
		Difficulty
		☆☆☆☆☆
		Overall Rating
		☆☆☆☆☆

Notes

HIKING LOG

Date

Hike/Trail Name	Location	

Start Time	End Time	Duration

Terrain	Elevation Gain/Loss	Distance

Gear	Food/Water	Onsite Facilities/Water
		Companions

Trail Conditions	Weather	Phone Reception/Carrier
	☀ ⛅ ☁ 🌬 / 💧 ⚡ ❄	
		Difficulty
		☆ ☆ ☆ ☆ ☆
		Overall Rating
		☆ ☆ ☆ ☆ ☆

Notes

HIKING LOG

Date:

Hike/Trail Name	Location	

Start Time	End Time	Duration

Terrain	Elevation Gain/Loss	Distance

Gear	Food/Water	Onsite Facilities/Water
		Companions

Trail Conditions	Weather	Phone Reception/Carrier
		Difficulty
		☆ ☆ ☆ ☆ ☆
		Overall Rating
		☆ ☆ ☆ ☆ ☆

Notes

HIKING LOG

		Date
Hike/Trail Name	Location	
Start Time	End Time	Duration
Terrain	Elevation Gain/Loss	Distance
Gear	Food/Water	Onsite Facilities/Water
		Companions
Trail Conditions	Weather	Phone Reception/Carrier
	☀ ⛅ ☁ 🌬 🌧 ⛈ ❄	
		Difficulty
		☆☆☆☆☆
		Overall Rating
		☆☆☆☆☆
	Notes	

HIKING LOG

Date

Hike/Trail Name	Location	
Start Time	End Time	Duration
Terrain	Elevation Gain/Loss	Distance
Gear	Food/Water	Onsite Facilities/Water
		Companions
Trail Conditions	Weather	Phone Reception/Carrier
		Difficulty
		☆ ☆ ☆ ☆ ☆
		Overall Rating
		☆ ☆ ☆ ☆ ☆

Notes

HIKING LOG

Date	

Hike/Trail Name	Location

Start Time	End Time	Duration

Terrain	Elevation Gain/Loss	Distance

Gear	Food/Water	Onsite Facilities/Water
		Companions

Trail Conditions	Weather	Phone Reception/Carrier
	☀ ⛅ ☁ 🌬 🌧 ⛈ ❄	
		Difficulty
		☆☆☆☆☆
		Overall Rating
		☆☆☆☆☆

Notes

HIKING LOG

Date

Hike/Trail Name	Location	
Start Time	End Time	Duration
Terrain	Elevation Gain/Loss	Distance
Gear	Food/Water	Onsite Facilities/Water
		Companions
Trail Conditions	Weather	Phone Reception/Carrier
		Difficulty
		☆☆☆☆☆
		Overall Rating
		☆☆☆☆☆
Notes		

 **HIKING LOG**	Date

Hike/Trail Name	Location

Start Time	End Time	Duration

Terrain	Elevation Gain/Loss	Distance

Gear	Food/Water	Onsite Facilities/Water
		Companions

Trail Conditions	Weather	Phone Reception/Carrier
		Difficulty
		☆ ☆ ☆ ☆ ☆
		Overall Rating
		☆ ☆ ☆ ☆ ☆

Notes

HIKING LOG

	Date

Hike/Trail Name	Location	

Start Time	End Time	Duration

Terrain	Elevation Gain/Loss	Distance

Gear	Food/Water	Onsite Facilities/Water
		Companions

Trail Conditions	Weather	Phone Reception/Carrier
		Difficulty
		☆ ☆ ☆ ☆ ☆
		Overall Rating
		☆ ☆ ☆ ☆ ☆

Notes

HIKING LOG

Date	

Hike/Trail Name	Location

Start Time	End Time	Duration

Terrain	Elevation Gain/Loss	Distance

Gear	Food/Water	Onsite Facilities/Water
		Companions

Trail Conditions	Weather	Phone Reception/Carrier
	☀ ⛅ ☁ 🌬 🌧 ⛈ ❄	
		Difficulty
		☆☆☆☆☆
		Overall Rating
		☆☆☆☆☆

Notes

HIKING LOG

	Date
Hike/Trail Name	**Location**
Start Time	**End Time**	**Duration**
Terrain	**Elevation Gain/Loss**	**Distance**
Gear	**Food/Water**	**Onsite Facilities/Water**
		Companions
Trail Conditions	**Weather**	**Phone Reception/Carrier**
		Difficulty ☆☆☆☆☆
		Overall Rating ☆☆☆☆☆
Notes		

HIKING LOG

Date

Hike/Trail Name	Location	

Start Time	End Time	Duration

Terrain	Elevation Gain/Loss	Distance

Gear	Food/Water	Onsite Facilities/Water
		Companions

Trail Conditions	Weather	Phone Reception/Carrier
	☀️ ⛅ ☁️ 🌬️ 🌧️ ⛈️ ❄️	
		Difficulty
		☆☆☆☆☆
		Overall Rating
		☆☆☆☆☆

Notes

HIKING LOG

Date

Hike/Trail Name	Location	

Start Time	End Time	Duration

Terrain	Elevation Gain/Loss	Distance

Gear	Food/Water	Onsite Facilities/Water
		Companions

Trail Conditions	Weather	Phone Reception/Carrier
		Difficulty
		☆ ☆ ☆ ☆ ☆
		Overall Rating
		☆ ☆ ☆ ☆ ☆

Notes

 **HIKING LOG**

		Date
Hike/Trail Name	Location	
Start Time	End Time	Duration
Terrain	Elevation Gain/Loss	Distance
Gear	Food/Water	Onsite Facilities/Water
		Companions
Trail Conditions	Weather	Phone Reception/Carrier
		Difficulty ☆☆☆☆☆
		Overall Rating ☆☆☆☆☆
Notes		

www.ingramcontent.com/pod-product-compliance
Lightning Source LLC
Chambersburg PA
CBHW071722020426
42333CB00017B/2363